D0585851

Famous People Famous Lives

Biographies of famous people to
support the curriculum.

Henry VIII

by Harriet Castor

Illustrations by Peter Kent

W
FRANKLIN WATTS
NEW YORK • LONDON • SYDNEY

First published in 1999 by
Franklin Watts
96 Leonard Street
London
EC2A 4XD

Franklin Watts Australia
14 Mars Road
Lane Cove
NSW 2066

ISBN: 0 7496 3530 4

A CIP catalogue record for this book
is available from the British Library.

Dewey Decimal Classification Number: 942.05

10 9 8 7 6 5 4 3 2 1

Series editor: Sarah Ridley
Consultant: Dr Anne Millard

Printed in Great Britain

Henry VIII

In 1501 there was a royal wedding in London. The King and Queen's eldest son, Prince Arthur, married a Spanish princess called Catherine of Aragon. Arthur's younger brother, Henry, led Catherine up the aisle.

What a fine young man!

Henry had grown up thinking he was going to be an important nobleman, or perhaps a powerful priest.

But five months after the wedding, Prince Arthur fell ill and died. Now Henry was the heir to the throne. His father made sure he was kept safe.

Then, when Henry was seventeen, his father died too. Henry became King Henry VIII.

One of the first things Henry did as king was to marry Catherine, the Spanish princess. Royal marriages were a good way of making an alliance, or friendship, between countries. Spain was an important and powerful country. Besides, Henry and Catherine liked each other.

Because Catherine was the widow of Henry's brother, Henry had to ask the Pope for special permission to marry her.
The Pope said yes.

Henry was everyone's idea of what a king should be. He was tall, handsome and sporty. He was good at languages and music. He loved hunting, dancing, feasting, and wearing fine clothes.

Government meetings bored Henry, and he hated writing letters. But he made sure his ministers told him everything that happened. They left all the most important decisions to him.

What is it, man? I'm going hunting.

Could you just sign this, Your Grace?

Henry's chief minister was a priest called Cardinal Wolsey. Unlike most people at Court, Wolsey hadn't been born into an important family.

Wolsey was clever and worked hard, and Henry trusted him. Many of the nobles were jealous of Wolsey's power. They especially hated him because he came from an ordinary family.

Wolsey's palace is magnificent.

Henry believed great kings should be great warriors, so he wanted to go to war. He decided to attack France, one of England's oldest enemies.

Henry sailed to France with his army. He didn't take part in the fighting himself, but his soldiers won a battle. Henry came home triumphant.

Soon the old French king died. The new king, François I, was young and athletic. Henry was curious to meet him, so Wolsey arranged it.

The meeting took place on the border between Calais – a town England owned then – and the rest of France. Everywhere was decorated with gold cloth, so people called the place 'The Field of the Cloth-of-Gold'.

Henry and Catherine had been married for nearly twenty years. They had had several children, but only one had survived: a daughter, Mary.

Henry wanted a son. He thought that only men were good at ruling countries.

Then Henry fell in love with one of Catherine's maids of honour, Anne Boleyn. She was young, witty and clever. He wanted to marry her.

Henry had begun to think that God was cross with him for marrying Catherine, his brother's widow. He wanted the new Pope to say that, in God's eyes, they had never truly been married.

The trouble was, Catherine's nephew Charles was the King of Spain. He was very powerful. The Pope knew if he agreed to do what Henry wanted, Charles would be angry.

The Pope made promises to both Charles and Henry. But he didn't keep them. Eventually, he sent a cardinal (an important priest) to England to judge the case for divorce. The cardinal he chose was old and ill.

When the case began, Catherine knelt at Henry's feet. She said she was his true wife. Then she left the courtroom and refused to come back.

Still there was no decision.
Henry was angry. He blamed
Wolsey and sent him to prison.
But Wolsey fell ill and died on
the way.

Then Anne Boleyn became
pregnant. Henry had to marry
her quickly so that the baby
could be next in line to the
throne.

So Henry's ministers persuaded Parliament to pass a law saying that *Henry* was head of the Church in England, and he could judge the divorce case himself. Henry divorced Catherine.

It's not up to the Pope. I'm divorced and that's that.

At this time, people all over Europe were arguing about the right way to worship God. One group, Catholics, supported the Pope. Another group, later called Protestants, were against the Pope. Many people were put to death.

Henry didn't like either side. He was against the Pope, but he was also against many things the Protestants believed in.

Henry wanted his subjects to believe only what he told them.

Henry ordered that every monastery and nunnery should be shut down. His new chief minister, Thomas Cromwell, organised it for him.

Henry said it was because the monks and nuns weren't living a holy life. They were greedy and lazy. This was true in some cases but not all. Many of the monasteries had lots of money and land, which Henry wanted.

Meanwhile, Anne had her baby. It was a girl, called Elizabeth. Henry was disappointed and cancelled his planned celebrations. He didn't know that Elizabeth would one day be a great ruler.

Still no son! God must think this marriage is wrong, too.

Anne got pregnant twice more, but lost the babies. Henry was angry. He had already fallen in love with someone else: one of Anne's ladies-in-waiting, called Jane Seymour.

Anne was put in prison. She was accused of plotting to murder Henry and of having affairs with several men. None of it was true, but Anne and the men had their heads chopped off. Straight afterwards, Henry married Jane.

The next year Jane had a baby boy, Edward. But Jane died a few days later. Henry was very sad.

Because royal marriages were a useful way of making friendships between countries, Thomas Cromwell started looking for a new wife for Henry right away.

Whenever a possible wife was suggested, Henry wanted to know what she looked like. So the famous painter, Hans Holbein, was sent to paint her.

One of the people Holbein
painted was the daughter of a
German duke – Anne of Cleves.

Henry agreed to marry Anne.
When she landed in England, he
was so impatient to meet her
that he arrived early, in disguise.

But Henry didn't like what he saw. He was angry with Cromwell for arranging the marriage.

Many of the nobles were glad.
They were jealous of Cromwell's
power and hated him because,
like Wolsey, he came from an
ordinary family.

Henry had already noticed a
new young woman at Court.
Her name was Katherine
Howard. The Howards were
powerful nobles who hated
Cromwell. They began plotting
against him.

Cromwell was put in the Tower of London. As Henry's minister, he had invented a new way for important prisoners to be executed without trial. It was used for the first time – on him.

Cromwell worked hard for Henry. Henry will regret this ...

Since Henry was Head of the Church, it was easy for him to divorce Anne of Cleves. Anne didn't argue. Henry gave her plenty of money to live on.

Now Henry was free to marry
his sweetheart, Katherine
Howard. She was five years
younger than Mary, Henry's
daughter. She was cheerful and
lively, but foolish, too.

Before her marriage, Katherine
had had several secret lovers.

She had fallen in love with an ambitious but charming courtier called Thomas Culpeper. Soon she started seeing him again.

Like every powerful family, the Howards had enemies. Some of them found out about Katherine's affair and told Henry. Henry was grief-stricken and furious. He had Katherine and her lover executed.

Bring me a sword! I'll kill her myself.

As his sixth wife Henry chose a young widow called Catherine Parr. She was intelligent, and kind to his children. She was also good at nursing Henry.

My leg is very sore today.

Even Catherine had enemies at Court. There was a plot against her, but she found out just in time. She rushed to Henry, and explained that her enemies had told him lies.

At last, aged fifty-five, Henry died. He was buried, as he'd ordered, next to Jane Seymour at Windsor Castle. Their son – the boy Henry had longed for – became King Edward VI.

More about Henry VIII

Rhyme to remember

There is a rhyme that makes it easy to remember what happened to each of Henry's six wives:

Divorced, beheaded, died,
Divorced, beheaded, survived.

Can you name them all (without looking back through the book?)

H&A, H&K, H&C, H&J

In Henry's time, royal buildings were often decorated with the initials of the king and queen. But Henry had so many queens that wood-carvers and window-makers were always having to change the initials. Sometimes the old initials survived. Today, if you go to

St James's Palace in London, for example, you can still see the initials of Henry and Anne Boleyn, who was only the second of his six wives.

Henry Tudor

Henry's family name was Tudor. His father, Henry VII, had been the first Tudor king. Henry VIII hoped that the Tudor family would reign for a long time. In fact, they lasted only as long as his children. All three became monarchs – as King Edward VI, Queen Mary I and Queen Elizabeth I. None of them had children of their own, so the Tudor line came to an end.